AMAZING PARENTING

All parents can be great parents, its a journey and we will get there

AMAZING PARENTING
Volume 1

By Grace Chukwu

Contents

Acknowledgments

I thank my God for always being there for me and giving me the strength to go on.

I love and appreciate my husband for being my friend, my confidante, my sound board, my allied force and standing by me through think, thin and very thin. Without him I couldn't be the parent that I am.

I adore my super children for not giving us any real trouble, for putting their hearts and minds to doing their best to make us proud.

I honour my dad for being a great single parent and my hero.

I must thank my Pastor, Matthew Ashimolowo for preaching and teaching the undiluted word of God.

I also want to acknowledge six wonderful women.

Amanda Agunsoye: My mentor and inspiration.

Lorna Lala, Kemi Osinowo, Susan Winner-Ogundele and Helen Creppy have been fanning my flames for the longest time.

Godlyn Chikwe: My prayer partner.

You six women have and continue to be my propellers. Your reward for your love and support towards me and my family can only come from above. God bless you!

Introduction

This book did not originally start out as a book. It was a collection of my thoughts in regards to all parents who needed a bit of guidance for the most powerful job in the world, bringing up children.

One day I began to write those thoughts down. And when I did; my husband read them and said 'you should put this in a book' and the rest is history as they say.

There are so many books on the market right now on the topic of parenting. Some of the books are good and interesting, many of them are long and give you deep meaning into parenting. If you are like me; when it comes to parenting I want support now and to the point. No nonsense.

This book is:

1. easy to read;

2. You know exactly what I'm talking about because there is nothing new under the sun when it comes to parenting, we've all been through it in one form or another;

3. I don't know about you but I don't have the time to read lengthy books and

4. Absolutely any parent can pick up this book; read it and implement what is needed for the required result.

This book could add value to your life long parenting and your children will thank you (not right away) for taking the time to be the best parent you could be for them and it is a pleasure and an honour to know I could have had a part to play in that great job by writing this book.

Many years ago while I was still in my twenties, I embarked on a life changing experience; called Camp America. Before I took the trip I did not know it would be life changing.

The camp catered for teen's right down to pre-schoolers. I had the pleasure of being the counsellor for the teenage girls. These girls came from the inner city of New York.

Some of their life stories they told me, left me wide eyed and mouth opened. In the short time I spent with the girls I grew fond of them and their families I never met.

I camped outside with the teenage girls, I mountain climbed with them, I swam with them, I had breakfast, lunch and dinner with them, I slept in the same wooden cabin with the them, I had deep meaningful conversation with them over camp fires and so much more.

When it was time for the girls to leave the camp and go home after two weeks. I cried as if they were my daughters. Then a new group of girls would arrive and I would do the same thing all over again - tears and all - for the entire summer.

It was there I realised that supporting parents and children in their families is what I wanted to do for the rest of my life.

From my experience, knowledge, work and research; I believe that parenting has three stages, all of which are aligned to the developmental stages of children.

Stage One, the sponge years; where your children soak up everything you do and say. Therefore you need to be the Manager.

Stage Two, the expressive years; where your children express their emotions, feelings and behaviours. Therefore you need to be the Adviser.

Stage Three, the winged stage; where your children find their wings and venture into the world. Therefore you need to be the Consultant.

As children develop through each stage, your style of parenting needs to develop as well. Each stage requires a different style of parenting. Regardless of the stage you are at; parenting should be amazing.

Chapter One

Chapter One

The Three Stages

Stage One.............Manager

Stage Two.............Adviser

Stage Three..........Consultant

Stage one - Manager

Between the ages of 0-12 years, your children need to be managed and taught by you - as the parent. They are watching you more closely than you think. Therefore, if there is anything you don't want your children to do or say, even throughout their childhood, this is the stage when you should not be caught doing it. Such as bad habits, smoking, drinking excessively or swearing. This will not be easy if you have been doing such since they were born.

Later on in the book I talk about not shouting at your children. Let me be honest with you. There were some mornings I would still be in bed and I would tell myself I was not going to shout today, but before I could even get one leg out of the bed, I had shouted at them for one reason or another. Parenting is a working progress; don't let anyone tell you otherwise.

There is an age old saying that states: *Life and death is in the power of the tongue.*

What this means is no matter what you are faced with, only speak positive about your children, even if they are being incredibly difficult. Saying negative things will not help the situation so why not say something positive?

You can kill your child's dreams and aspirations with your words or you can give them wings with your words. You choose.

I have noticed and I'm sure you have, too, there are five (possibly more) basic levels of care that all children require.

1. Food
2. Adequate Shelter
3. Access to Education
4. Access to Medical services
5. Emotional Warmth

If you are administering these five, you are onto a good start.

When your child was born, you instantly became a leader, whether you believe it or not. What kind of a leader kind of leader is what you will have to determine. Here is where you may find out how much emotional intelligence you have. This is simply being in tune with your children's emotions as well as your own.

Set rules and boundaries early on in this stage because trying to get through rules and boundaries in stage two or three is a nightmare to say the least. Integrity teaching is good here as well.

Integrity is huge; especially in this time we are living in. To teach a child to do the right thing when no one is looking; is priceless. You may not be able to teach your child long division and verbal reasoning; but you will not go wrong if all you teach them integrity.

Routine, routine again I say routine. Get this in early on, children simply work better, respond better and act better when there is structure and routine in their lives. It's a fact.

You manage what they do, where they go and what they wear and almost everything else. You teach your children manners respect, and honour. The educational system may help in these areas but ultimately this is your responsibility.

Gone are the days when we (society) can blame the government or the school system for what simply is poor parenting. (I will come back to poor parenting later on). There is not a government on the face of this earth that can legislate morality. We parents have to instil it.

If you consider the condition of the youth and their families in this country, many of them are in a dire position.

Good parenting is the number one key for solid family live.

Good parenting also solves the problems, dilemmas and issues of children caught in the web of no direction for their lives, lack of vision and no aspirations.

As we know, one of the major pillars in a country is its families and once the family structure begins to decay the social frame of society begins to fragment.

Many families are under attack, with absent fathers, (and mothers), drug and alcohol problems and out of control teens. There is a solution and that is to be the parent your children and society needs!

Backing down and giving in is a big no - no. This is the stage where you stand your ground, let your yes be yes and your no be no. *"Parents who are afraid to put their foot down usually have children who step on their toes". (Chinese Proverb).*

I know firsthand putting your foot down can be hard. It's a power struggle and your children may think they have the power.

When our daughter was two going on three years; she would not eat what the rest of the family would eat. She would insist on eating food that did not need much chewing it seemed.

So to keep the peace and have an easy life I would cook two dinners - one for me, my husband and son, and something different for our daughter. If I tried to feed her what we were eating she would cry, throw up, and purse her lips together. To be honest with you, it was easier to give in and give in and give her what she wanted. Until..........

As a family, we love our Sunday roast and we would have this every weekend, except for our daughter. She would have something else that I would have to prepare, or she would not eat anything at least that's what I thought, or let her lead me to believe.

We came home one Sunday afternoon and my husband was sorting out the children while I went straight into the kitchen to make dinner. I had already cook the meat in the morning; I just had to put the vegetables on to boil and put the potatoes in the oven. Then I would make something for our daughter to eat.

This particular Sunday my husband came into the kitchen to see what was taking so long and could see I was making two dinners. My husband said there and then, "That's it; she eats what we eat". He fed our daughter that day, and of course she made a big fuss but in the end she ate what we ate.

However, whenever I tried to feed her; she would not eat. But I persevered and put my foot down long enough to show her who was boss. And ever since then, I only cook one dinner for the family. Now she eats whatever we eat.

You may find the power struggle throughout your parenthood but, as the parent, you should always keep the reins of the power.

The so-called wanting an "easy life" now, will only result in drudgery as your children get older. Deal with what needs to be dealt with now!

When your children are little and cute, it is easy to gloss over negative behaviour; after all they are little and cute. However there will come a day when your little cute 'Johnny' will be bigger than you, stronger than you and have more "lip" then you. The cute factor soon wears off.

In this stage stability and consistency is key, and consistency in all things; that means in discipline and in having fun. Your children need to see both sides of you - it's good for them and it's good for you.

At this stage, if you see any undesirable behaviour, this is the time you nip it in the bud. What seems cute in the early stages; quickly looses it cuteness when that same child becomes a teen. e.g. telling you "no".

Also during this stage, your children need to see lots of you, hear lots of you, and feel lots of you, (warmth/ affection).

This is when you set the emotional atmosphere of your home with love.

This is the time when you teach your children a strong work ethic. "What you want, you work for", and "always aim high" are both great ethics to teach. This ensures that your children mature into adults who understand working towards achievements.

Pocket money and the art of saving money can be introduced at this stage, for whatever reason you see fit. For my husband and I, pocket money was never an issue because we didn't give pocket money to our children just because it was the end of the week or because they had tidied their rooms.

Of course, we always gave them dinner money and money for school trips etc. However, we only gave them pocket money for excellent achievements, in academics or sports.

Sometimes, I would give them each a sweet, and who ever kept their sweet in their mouths the longest, would get money. You don't have to be serious all the time you are giving your children money; it can be for fun things too.

This is where you identify your children effortless advanced ability; in other words, a natural gift of '"God-given talent". All children have something they can do with ease. Hone in and focus on this, and endeavour to develop this gift.

Our son is into football big time and I can't begin to tell you how much money we have spent on football boots, not to mention the endless cold Sunday mornings watching him play and then having to get changed in the car and rush to church.

It is imperative that you are into what your children are into. Our daughter is into tennis, and she is also doing very well academically. We endeavour to pay for extra tuition for maths and English lessons for her. Your commitment to their gift is their fuel.

The fun factor is established in this stage. Whatever constitutes fun for you as a family – whether it is sport, board games, walks in the woods, bowling or just watching a family DVD - do lots of it. This stage is where bonds are made and foundations for future relationships are made or broken.

Stage one is the perfect time to introduce house work to your children. It does not need to be heavy duty e.g. cleaning windows or scrubbing decking. Simply have them pick up their shoes, keep their rooms tidy, make their beds before leaving the house and keeping their dirty clothes in one place; ready for them to bring to the washing machine when you ask.

Trying to introduce house work to teenagers will be more of a chore for you than for them.

Children are the same the world over, whether their black, white, European, Asian, American or African, rich, poor, educated or uneducated; they all want what they want - and preferably now. It is your parenting that will make the difference.

Here is not where you lower your standards, but you explain your standards. Most parents have standards that they hold dear to their hearts. It is important that your children know what they are and run with them into adulthood.

In this stage leading by example is crucial. If you are not leading by example; you are just not leading. The ultimate goal of a parent is to see their children mature into confident, well rounded adults who can sustain themselves and a happy successful family. Almost everything they do will be because of your example or lack of it.

There are two things that your children will do for you - embarrass you or make you proud. The great thing about that statement is you have a huge input into which one they do most.

I would like to interject here the age-old saying "spare the rod and spoil the child". Should we be beating our children with rods? No, again I say no. The "rod" can be translated to mean; discipline. So whatever you use for disciplining your child e.g., naughty step, time out, remove Xbox or grounding for one week - that is your "rod". Use it and use it well.

I mentioned poor parenting earlier, and I will be a little controversial here, don't get mad with me; I'm on your side.

ADHD (Attention deficit hyperactivity disorder) Vs Poor Parenting?

What!! I here you shriek.

When our son was a little boy, he was all over the place and I mean, all over. We would tell him off, sit him down, play all over the place with him, and sometimes we could not wait for him to fall asleep. He had all the signs of a child with ADHD.

This went on for years. My husband and I would notice he was different from the children in play school; he had more energy than most of them. When we took him out in the buggy, he would always want to run off. At home, he did what he wanted.

Did he have ADHD? No, he did not. We just had to persevere with our rules and boundaries, and engaging him with what he enjoyed doing. Now, "all that all over the place" business is expressed on the football field, to the extent he was top goal score three seasons running and he won a trophy from school for running cross country.

Many children show signs of ADHD, especially boys, do we really want to drug them to be calm? By all means, take your child to the Doctor if you have suspicions, but please endeavour to ride it out, don't throw in the towel just because it's hard work.

The time and effort that you put in at this stage is an investment that is generational; for your children, grandchildren and even your great grandchildren.

Take your mind back to when your children were conceived. Whether the event was a mistake or on purpose, they are here now. You cannot afford to fail as a parent; like you can afford to fail at Maths, pottery classes, your driving test or painting and decorating.

Failing at these ventures is not life-affecting; parenting is. But there is good news. If you did not do a good job of being a good parent yesterday there is always today to be better.

Attachment with your children at this time is crucial

(Attachment theory; read books by Professor Shemmings and other authors on the subject).

During my research I came across Diane Baumrind, a 1960's psychologist who conducted a study on more than 100 pre-school age children. She identified four important dimensions of parenting.

1. Authoritarian Parenting:

These kinds of parents expect their children to follow strict rules, 'simply because I say so'. These parents have high demands but are not engaging with their children.

2. Authoritative Parent:

These parents like the authoritarian parent have rules and boundaries; however this parent is more democratic. They are responsive to their children and listen to their questions. These parents are more nurturing and forgiving.

3. Permissive Parenting:

Permissive parents are the ones who let their children get away with behaviours that 1 and 2 parents would not. These parents are indulgent parents; they have few demands to make on their children. These parents rarely discipline their children and therefore have a low expectation of maturity and self control. Baumrind states that these parents are non traditional, lenient and avoid confrontation. This parent is more of a friend to their children than a parent.

4. Uninvolved Parent:

An uninvolved parenting style is characterised by few demands, low responsiveness and little communication. While these parents fulfil their child's basic needs, they are generally detached from their child's life. In extreme cases, these parents may even reject or neglect the needs of their children.

These four Parenting Styles are theories. However, number two sounds worth pursuing.

If you have more than one child, you are all too familiar with hearing the words "I'm telling", as your head slowly rolls back, and your hand comes up to your forehead and then rubs your eyes. Your child comes into your presents and says "muuuum....."Or '"daaaaaaad....."

All children need one-to-one time with you, especially if they have a sibling or two. Give each child half an hour to an hour of your undivided attention, once a week every week, as a minimum. This may be challenging if you are a one parent family but not impossible.

Let your child choose the activity for the set time, and just go with the flow. It could be fairy cake making, a board game, rough and tumble sit and chat or just about anything; but the key is your attention is only on that child for that time.

You will quickly see your children won't clamber for your attention all at once, because they know they will have their one-to-one time with you.

I would like to touch a little on single dads. At the beginning of this book I thank my dad for being my hero. If you are a single dad reading this book; be encouraged.

My dad was a single parent and he did a remarkable job, in my eyes. As far as I was concerned, he was all I needed. I will never forget the time he took me to Holloway in London to buy me my brownie uniform, and another time he came to watch me in a gymnastics competition, and all the times we made cakes together.

At the time, these events did not seem like big deals. But now I'm a mum with a husband and less children than he had, I'll never know how he juggled everything. He is truly a gift from God to me.

It takes an exceptional dad to want to keep his children, without his wife or partner. It takes an extraordinary dad to work full time and care for his children, and it takes a great dad to just hang in there for the long haul. You are doing a superb job single dad!

Towards the end of stage one, or even early on, you will know through body language which of your children is the touchy-feely one, which is the "don't hug or kiss me" one, and which the girly girl is. Use these traits to help you interact with your children; it may surprise you how they respond.

Stage two - Adviser

I have worked with teenagers and children periodically since 1995 and I have taken the time to observe them.

Between the ages of 13-17, you become your children's adviser. This is where you, as the parent, sit and discuss all topics with your children, advising and discussing their opinion, and letting them know your standpoint on each topic.

It may surprise you to know there are parents out there that are not having any problems with their teens. Why? Because you have to keep them busy and active from an early age.

In these years, your child may have seen, heard and done more than you did when you were the same age. In this stage, you compromise and negotiate more, but never lower your standards.

Your children are now of an age where you can not totally control everything they do. This stage needs as much love, attention and encouragement as stage one. In this stage, you spend a lot more time listening.

When our son crossed over into this stage, I could not believe he was a teen already, and so much of what we had been through in stage one was now paying off.

Did he give us attitude? Did he say "my friends are allowed to do that"? Did he back chat? Yes he did. All things I would not have dreamed of saying to my dad when I was a teen.

As a parent, you have to know when your child is being expressive and when they are being rude. Never tolerate rudeness from your children - ever. But there are times when your children will want to express themselves, but it comes across as rude because of their body language or tone. You know your child, so you should quickly be able to decipher the difference.

Let your children know your love is unconditional. One day our son came home from school and informed me he only got a certain amount in his test, and his grade for that particular test was not that high.

I asked my son "Did you study for the test? He said "yes" I asked him, did you try your best in the test? He said "yes" and I told him, "That's all I want from you and your sister, to always try your best".

Not only did he feel better for our little chat, I believe it resonated to him, it's him I love not the good grades.

Avoid the temptation to "baby" your child. It is easy to look at your child and see that baby you had; what seemed like yesterday, and want to treat them as such. Not only are you going backwards but your child's confidence and self-esteem may be compromised if done on a regular basis.

In stage one, your children listens to you based on your authority as their parent.

Stage two is based on your authority and negotiation; your children are having more input from the outside world.

Allow me to talk a little about negotiation. Imagine driving your car through a normal size road. You can maintain constant speed. Now imagine going through a road width restriction. You automatically slow down and negotiate the space provided, why? Because you don't want to damage your car.

It is the same is with your child at this stage. You could give your child an instruction in stage one without having to "slow down" because they trust your authority e.g. "Hold mummy's hand as we cross the road".

In stage two when you give your child an instruction, they may trust your authority but because they are also getting input from other sources, you "slow down" and negotiate i.e. talk, so not to damage your relationship.

I would like to interject here parents don't be afraid of your children's questions, because if you are, they will find out somewhere else. And I assure you, Google is not the best parent. Engage your child in conversation and if they don't bring up topics such as sex, drugs and bullying, then you bring them up and talk for as long as they want, you can always bring up the topics another time.

Follower or a leader? We all would like our children to follow our instructions, or the instructions of those in authority. However in this stage, we need to be teaching our children how to be a leader when it comes to not giving into peer pressure.

That means not following friends to do the wrong thing e.g. to steal, lie, bunk school etc. This can be very difficult for teens, but it will easier if you have taught them to be a leader, even if that means just to lead themselves to do the right thing. That can be the difference between good grades and bad grades, which then snowballs into bigger and better out comes.

Well, I hear you ask, how do you teach teens to be leaders? Chapter Two will help you, but in a nut shell simply flood their beings with praise and correction. Tilt the scales a little more on the praise side and let them know you always have an open door policy; even for those bottom lip-biting questions and confessions.

For some teens talking is a chore. But as I said before, you know your child. Take opportunities to bring up conversation if they don't, remember not every discussion has to be deep and meaningful; you can just chat. It is sometimes during those chats that they bring up the deep meaningful subjects.

Here is where your leading by example rings true, particularly when your child leaves school and gets discouraged by job hunting or not wanting to go to college. If you are a parent not working or in some sort of further education yourself, you will find it increasingly difficult to get your seventeen year old out of bed if *you* have nothing to get out of bed for.

Your children may never know your true worth until they themselves become parents. So avoid pointless frustrations with them when they fail to see and have insight of all you do for them. Know this, delayed gratification is sweet.

If you have been a good manager, stage two should not be too much of a struggle for you. If you are reading this book and you have passed stage one and two and it was a struggle, how do you ensure the next stage is better?

Simply recognise where you went wrong, don't blame anyone, take responsibility, make amends, listen to sound advice when it comes to parenting and move on.

Stage three – Consultant

Between the ages of 18 - 20 and beyond, you as the parent become your children's consultant. At this stage you sit down with your children and give them your wisdom and experience on life.

You then allow them to make their own choices and live with the consequence of those choices that they have made.

A wise person once said, "Children spell love T I M E."

Time is a huge factor in all three stages but in varying degrees; get the balance right and you will reap the benefit.

If you have been a good manager and a good adviser; stage three should be 'OK'.

There will be times in all three stages you have to let go and let your children explore, even though your heart might be beating ten to the dozen. This is where all your teaching, training and influence come into play.

You, your spouse/partner and children are a team and you all have respective roles to play, just like in a real game of sport. It is important that all roles are established and recognised by all inside and outside your family. Each member of your team must know their role from early on, and be committed to the success of the team (family).

You may be a conventional family consisting of mum, dad and 2.4 children, or you could be grandparents bringing up grandchildren; whatever your composition, you are a team - never forget it.

No matter how old your children are, they have three rules to follow. They are to have - : 1, manners, 2, respect and 3, honour - for you, themselves and humanity.

If your daughter follows these three rules, it would be near impossible for her to be abused by anyone.

If your son follows these three rules he could be a pillar in society.

In all three stages, you may encounter bumps, cracks and pot holes along the way. However, as on any normal journey; you do not give up because you have met these obstacles on the road. You continue to your destination. There is a destination for parenting, and you will get there victoriously.

Many moons ago, I worked in a young mum's hostel. This meant the mums where the same age and younger than stage three children. It was a wonderful experience for me, working in the hostel. I would support the mums with life skills and working with them to get back into school, Start College or into employment.

If you are a young parent reading this book, you are also to be encouraged. Now you have children please don't feel all doors are closed to you, on the contrary, if you did not have any dreams before your children were born, this is the time to have them and fulfil them. A wise person once said "if you want a better future for your children, show them the way by making a better future for yourself."

Only you can decide whether having a baby so young is a hindrance or a help, makes you bitter or better, stronger or weaker.

Studies show that Parents are increasingly involved in their Millennials' decisions (A Millennial is a child born between 1982- early 2000s). According to one study, more than a third of Millennials' with a mentor say a parent fills that role. In another study, when asked to list the most influential people in their lives, 61% named their parents ahead of political leaders, news media, teachers, coaches, faith leaders and celebrities.

Pew Research Centre, based in Washington reports that 36% of Millennials still live at home with their parents.

So, as you can see from these studies, there are many children in this age bracket who hold us [parents] in high regard.

Your parents may have failed you in stages one, two or three, but that does not mean you have to with your children.

Implement the principals of this book into your parenting with an open mind, and an open heart, and an honest mouth.

Failure to utilise each window of the parenting stages will make the next stage even harder to accomplish, leaving you with the task of having to play catch-up. As we all know, playing catch-up in life can be detrimental to us as parents and to our children.

Whether you are a married parent, cohabiting parent, single parent or a step parent, you owe it to the children you care for to be the best parent.

Hopefully, this book will give you tips, tools, ideas, strategies and help towards your life long parenting journey.

This is personal to me and my husband, and I would like to share it with you. No matter where our children are; on the spectrum of childhood, and no matter where we've been on the spectrum of parenthood, we have found that prayer changes things. It has been an instrument that has backed us up in the most difficult times.

In your parenting life time, you will be faced with heart-wrenching, back breaking and sleep-swallowing decisions. In the face of such times, the only thing that will work is to get on your knees and pray; just like you would if you were in a plan that was about to crash. No-one would blame you for praying.

Ultimately, we want our children to take care of us in our old age, whether that be financially, physically or just pop round for a cup of cappuccino. We want them in our lives forever, and the only way they are going to want us in their lives forever is for us to be the best parents we can be.

Explanation of three chapters:

Chapters Two, Three and Five need a little explaining, due to them being for you and your children to explore.

Chapter Two. Relationship Building with Teens and Parents.

This deals with the ups and downs of your relationship with your teenager. There are parts of the chapter for you to discuss with your teen and support them in this area.

Chapter Three. Leadership Skills for Teens.

This tackles the possibility of you bringing the leadership skills out in your teen. This chapter is for you to share together, after you have gone through it first, and recognised the potential for your teen to be a leader.

Chapter Five. Don't Groom Me.

Chapter Five is what I call the safety chapter. As a parent or someone who cares for children, you know the dangers children face. We are living in a society where children are targets for many unsavoury characters, to say the least. This chapter is for you to explain some of those dangers to your children, one of them being the Groomer.

Chapter Two

Chapter Two

Relationship Building with Teens and Parents

As I said earlier this chapter is for you and your teen.

1 Anger Management In The Home

2 How You Communicate Love

3 What Do You Do When You Mess Up (As A Teen)

4 Share Dreams And Visions

5 Talking About Difficult Subjects

6 Speak Positively About Each Other

1. Anger Management in the Home

In any relationship, there are ups and downs. Even in my own relationship with my children, anger can arise. Anger is a natural human emotion that you have and express. There is nothing wrong with being angry but how we behave toward others when we are angry is a different matter.

It is important to have strategies in place to deal with such situations. (Further down I talk about ground rules).

Unacceptable anger expression, however, includes shouting, swearing, hurting others or yourself physically or emotionally. The implications and consequences of such behaviour can result in fighting, becoming an outcast, loss of relationships, criminal record, imprisonment and in the worst case scenario - death.

What to do when you feel anger arising. Anger can arise very quickly, but there are signs beforehand that you recognise. It is not acceptable to say "that's the way I am" or "I can't help it"

Before anger ever arises, parents and teens need to set ground rules for anger management i.e.

Give each other space to calm down

Have bricks and a hammer in the garden to smash up

Scream into a pillow

Count to ten

Go to a room alone and shout

Go for a run

Or anything else you wish to do without causing harm.

Once these ground rules are set and the house hold has been made aware of them, it will make matters a lot easier when anger arises.

As soon as you (the teen) recognise the signs of anger arising, in a low toned firm voice -

without aggression - let the person who you are angry at know you need space away from the situation to calm down. When anger dies down then conversation can resume.

A standoff is what you (the parent) want to avoid. If you find yourself in a head-to-head battle with your teenager, this is a lose- lose situation. In this instance, you as the parent need to stand down and give your teen a chance to think through what you have said. Leave them alone for a while, and go back calmly giving the original instruction.

Before I leave this chapter I must emphasise that standing down and backing down are two different actions entirely. To back down means to give in and let your teen have their way. For example, you ask your teen to wash up and they refuse. Backing down would be you then doing the washing up yourself.

(Wrong move).

The consequences of you backing down; leads your teen to believe they are right all the time and they should be left alone to do whatever they want. When a child grows up thinking they can have what they want, when they want it, and do what they want, eventually when it's time for that child to face the real world, their coping mechanism for restraint and self-control is nonexistent. This could lead down a slippery, path of destruction.

To stand down is a military term. When two opposing soldiers have drawn their weapons on each other, one has to stand down to give the opportunity for peace.

In a parent and teen situation, your teen may not be mature enough to stand down or does not want to lose face, or they are embarrassed or just hormonal. By you standing down, it lets your teen have a moment to think about what you have said and the consequence of disobeying you. This then also opens the avenue for a peace talk (wise move).

When working as a couple (mum and dad), team work is key. Even if you are a blended family with step-siblings or step-parents, your voices must be as one. You must be singing from the same hymn sheet. Don't allow your children to play you off one another.

Now, there are many reasons your teen may be angry, and this will need addressing at some point. Reasons can range from absent dad or mum, peer pressure, feeling no-one understands them, rejection and the list goes on.

If you have a child with behavioural issues and you find yourself constantly at logger head with them - possibly due to unspoken secrets, loss of a loved one, or abandonment – at the same point you will have to discuss "what's 'wrong". But you may have to seek professional support.

Due to the constraints of the book, I am unable to go into what could be the factors that have lead to such behaviour. There is no quick fix, and in those cases I would possibly need to be with you physically to help you unravel the past.

However, be encouraged. I have a saying: "Where there is breath, there is hope."

2. How You Communicate Love

We all work, operate, and function better when understood. How you communicate to others may not be the way others communicate, so you need to learn how they want to be communicated with. A powerful communication tool is love.

Parent(s): ask your teen how they want you to communicate love. And teen: ask your parent how they want you to communicate love back. This exercise is very informative and enriching for both parties. With the information gathered, implement immediately and watch your communication levels grow.

For instance, a parent may want their teen to show them love by listening to instructions and to do it without an attitude. On the other hand the teen may want their parent to show them love by not "freaking out" at the slightest thing the teen says or does.

3. What Do You Do When You Mess Up (as a teen)

Accept responsibility

Everybody makes mistakes, so you will make mistakes and do things you regret. However, you must hold your hand up and accept responsibility. It is the right thing to do and the mature thing to do.

Tell the truth

When you mess up, there is a tendency to lie and cover the truth. This is a wrong move and should be avoided at all cost, however, once the truth is out the mending can begin.

Say sorry to those you hurt
You cannot take back the wrong you have done, but you can let those you have hurt know that you regret your actions, by sincerely saying sorry. I know saying sorry can be hard because you are admitting you were wrong, but once you've said it, you can move on.

Recognise where you went wrong and learn from it
The greatest inventors went wrong and failed many times, but today we have traffic lights, and light bulbs, and many other inventions as a result.

Making mistakes is a great way to learn what not to do, as long as you don't keep on making the same mistakes.

Ask for help early on before things get out of hand

Asking for help is not a sign of weakness and it can save you a lot of heart ache and shame. Asking for help shows maturity and humility - attributes you need going through life.

4. Share Dreams and Visions

It is important to have dreams and visions of things you want to see happen in the future. Once you know each other's dreams and visions, it makes it easy to know and understand where the other one wants to be.

Parent(s): sit down with your teen and both of you talk about and write down your dreams and visions. e.g., move house, get married, pass driving test, go to university, go on holiday, etc. Also, write down how you intend to reach these dreams and visions.

Set time frames and measurements for each one. Write down as many as you want; it does not matter how big or small the dreams are.

Every three or six months, sit down together and go through your dreams and visions and see how far you have come.

This is a great and effective way to build bonds between parent and teens.

5. Talking About Difficult Subjects

At times, you will have things that need discussing that are difficult or embarrassing.

The first thing to put in place is for the atmosphere be conducive for such conversations i.e. quiet, private and calm.

Let your teen / parents know this conversation is sensitive and you need their undivided attention. Then begin to talk about the subject.

The listener should let the communicator finish what they are saying before asking questions or interrupting.

The listener is not to fly off the handle, no matter what has been said. The communicator is to give the listener a moment or two to process the information. In some cases - depending on the subject - may need a longer period of time to process.

Both listener and communicator, depending on the subject must show empathy.

6. Speak Positively About Each Other

Words are powerful and we should always think before we speak, because once the words are out you can never take them back.

It is a proven fact that positive feedback and positive encouragement helps you to grow emotionally. It has been said that even talking positively to plants - as opposed to negatively - helps them grow and flourish.

When you speak positively to your teen, you are creating an atmosphere for security and happiness. e.g., you look nice, I love you, well done, you are a big help, I appreciate you, etc. A warm hug always goes down well with nice words.

If done on a day-to-day basis, it will build your relationship with each other. Both speaker and receiver will enjoy a sense of well being and acceptance.

All six steps will work but will take effort, time and most of all patience.

Chapter Three

Chapter Three

Leadership Skills for Teens

(Parents are to assist their teen in this chapter)

1. Lead Yourself

2. Rule The World

3. Check Out Your Friends

4. Be Brave

5. Problem Solver

6. Perfect

1. Lead Yourself

Leadership is a skill that can be learned and taught. Why is leadership important? There are so many "pulls" in this life, and if you don't lead yourself correctly, you will be pulled in the wrong direction.

When you can lead yourself to do good, in spite of inside and outside pressures, you are ready to lead. You will always have the opportunity to do wrong, but a leader **chooses** to do good.

2. Rule the World

To be a leader you don't have to rule the world but you do need to rule "your" world. A leader is in control of what he or she does, and when they do it. They are not led by the crowd; instead they influence the crowd to do the right thing.

Your attitude plays an important part in your leading. Attitude determines your altitude; in other words, it is your attitude that will take you up and cause people to follow you there.

Being a leader means you lead by example, therefore you have to be in control of your emotions and urges, doing the right thing at the right time is vital.

3. Check Out Your Friends

Your friends help give you identity. If you maintain bad friends, it is only a matter of time before you turn bad. Being a leader means the friends you keep enhance your leadership, not undermine it.

Don't be mistaken. A leader is not someone who leads a mob to do evil; that someone is a dictator.

EXERCISE: Go through your mobile phone contacts, Face book etc., and write a list and see how many of your friends encourage you to do good and how many of your friends encourage you to do bad. For example, which friends would tell you to go to school if you wanted to bunk off, and which ones would encourage you to lie or steal? A wise man once told me, there are four kinds of friends.

1. Subtract Friend,

2. Multiply Friend,

3. Divide Friend and

4. Add Friend.

1. The Subtract friend drains you of energy, takes your money, and generally leaves you empty and depleted.

2. The Divide friend always causes arguments between you and them or you and your friends, they back-stab and lie.

3. The Multiply friend increases your capacity in good areas i.e. education, good friendships, good ideas and so on.

4. The Add friend is someone who brings you joy and makes you laugh, they also are not scared to tell you when you are not doing the right thing or taking the wrong path.

The last two kinds of friends are the ones that you should have in your life.

Compartmentalise these friends, and see how many you have on your good list and how many on your bad list. Then you decide if you want to keep them as friends or not.

4. Be Brave

Being a leader means you have to be brave. In society today, there are issues like under-age sex, drugs, alcohol abuse and violence; that's made to look cool, but in reality these issues are devastating to lives.

Being a leader means standing up for what is right, even though peer pressure is the opposite to what's right. You may have to stand alone on many issues, but that is what makes a good leader.

5. Problem Solver

What keeps a leader leading is the problems they solve. Be a problem solver. When your friends come to you with issues, tell them the right thing to do, or help them find out where they can get their problem solved.

Problem solving is what defines salaries, positions, opportunities, access, and the list goes on and on. Problem solving is a great attribute to a leader.

6. Perfect

Being a leader does not mean you are perfect. Being a leader does not mean you know it all. Always ask for help and advice from the right sources. You will make mistakes, but a good leader always owns up to their mistakes, says sorry, and learns from them.

All six steps work, however all six steps need working on.

Chapter Four

Chapter Four

Parent(s) to Set Rules and Boundaries (R&B)

1. Parent(s) To Agree And Write Out Rules And Boundaries
2. Discuss R&B With The Children
3. Always Follow Through
4. Parent(s) Discuss Disagreements In Private Away From The Children
5. Parent(s) Don't Get Into Shouting Match With Children
6. Pick Your Fights
7. Let The Punishment Fit The Crime

1. Parent(s) to Agree and Write Out Rules and Boundaries

Children, from a very young age, benefit from being taught rules and boundaries. This helps them later in life to become well- rounded and law abiding citizen. If parents fail to do this, many children grow up unruly and bad- mannered to say the least.

Once parents have agreed the R&B for their home, these need to be implemented immediately.

2. Discuss R&B with the Children

Children need to have things explained to them in terms they can understand. Once your children know your R&B, and more importantly the consequences for breaking them then you can put them in place.

Write the R&B out and put them in a place where the children can see them - in their room, on the fridge, or anywhere you deem fit.

3. Always Follow Through

Once the R&B have been set, your children will test you; knowingly or unknowingly. For the R&B to be effective you as parent(s) must follow through at all times.

If children know they can get away with breaking the R&B without any consequence you will be fighting a losing battle. STAND YOUR GROUND.

4. Parents Discuss Disagreements in Private Away from the Children

There may be times as parents you don't see eye -to-eye or you are not working as a team. It is very important that the children are shielded from your disagreements, especially if they escalate to shouting and arguing. Always discuss "hot" topics in private. If the children feel or see that they can play you off of each other they will. i.e. if mum grounds Johnny, dad must back mum up - even if he does not agree. Mum and dad should later discuss this out of ear shot to Johnny.

Parents who constantly shout and arguing at each other while children are present or in the vicinity, can affect their children's development.

5. Parent(s) Don't Get into a Shouting Match with Children

There is a power struggle that takes place when parent(s) and children shout at each other. As the parent(s) you must at all times maintain the power; never in an aggressive manner, but firm and to the point.

Once you lose the power struggle with your children, it is very hard to gain it back. Give your instructions once or twice in a low firm voice and walk away. If they continue to shout; calmly remind them of the consequences. I once heard someone say "if you lose your cool you lose your power."

6. Pick Your Fights

As a parent, you must refrain from coming down hard for every little thing your children do. If it is not an R&B issue, let it go. Children still need room to express themselves without being "jumped on."

If you '"fight" every little thing they do, when they do something wrong that deserves a telling off, they will not see the seriousness of it because you **always** tell them off.

7. Let the Punishment Fit the Crime

All crime needs punishment; however you wouldn't put a man in jail for life for stealing a loaf of bread.

When your children break the R&B - and they will - It is not beneficial for you to read them the riot act if they have done something small e.g. spilt the milk, or forgot to make their bed.

Let your punishment have stages: if they break big R&B let the punishment be of a higher grade; and if they break small R&B, let the punishment be of a lesser grade.

Always explain why they are being punished. And once the punishment is over give them the chance to say sorry and move on.

All seven steps will work but will take time, effort and most of all patience.

Chapter Five

Chapter Five

DON'T GROOM ME

(Parents to assist their children in the chapter)

1. What Does A Groomer Look Like?

2. What Does A Groomer Say?

3. What Does A Groomer Want?

4. Where does A Groomer Hang Out?

5. Never Never Never

6. What Do I Do?

1. What Does A Groomer Look Like?

A groomer can be male or female, a stranger, pose as a friend, a relative, or a neighbour.

They can be rich or poor and they can be someone you've known a long time.

2. What Does A Groomer Say?

A groomer may want you to keep secrets, they may want you to lie for them, they may threaten you (don't' tell or else). They may say they love you. They may not say anything like that for a long time.

3. What Does A Groomer Want?

A Groomer wants power over you, they want to abuse you, and they want to make you do things for <u>their</u> pleasure. Possibly, they want to do you serious physical harm.

4. Where Does A Groomer Hang out?

A Groomer can be found at home, in the park, on holiday, at school and on the internet. They could be anywhere.

5. Never Never Never

Never be alone with such a person, never let them touch you and never keep their secrets.

6. What do I Do?

If this has happened to you or someone you know - whether it happened in the past or is happening now- what you should do is tell a parent, teacher, the police, social services or Child Line.

Chapter Six

Chapter Six

How To Say "No" Without Feeling Bad

1. The Word No

2. Firm But Calm

3. Discuss The No

4. Disobey The No

5. Stand Your Ground

1. The Word No

The word no is not a swear word nor a bad word. You need to enforce the word no in your children's life for them to be rounded and grounded in society. Hearing no from you as their parent puts them in good stead for hearing no in the future by another authority figures i.e. teachers, police, bosses and so on.

No is a word that needs to be said; to protect and to teach, amongst other things. Hearing no as a child can be annoying for them, but as a parent it needs to be said. The more you flinch from saying no, the more rebellious your children will become.

2. Firm But Calm

No is not a fighting word. Never shout it or use it aggressively. It's a word that should lead to a discussion (depending on the age of your children). There is nothing wrong with explaining why you have said no. Your children may badger you to change your no to a yes.

Be firm but calm. Let your no be final

3. Discuss The No

When you say no to your child, be prepared to discuss the no. Try to refrain from having an argument about it, but sit down and express your concern.

In your discussion set out consequences and punishment if the no is disobeyed. However don't stifle your child's expression; allow them to politely challenge your no. If your children do challenge the no, it does not mean you should change it to a yes.

4. Disobey The No

If your child still insists on disobeying you, then reinforce the consequences and punishment you have discussed. Let the punishment fit the severity of the no. Do not go overboard with the punishment.

5. Stand Your Ground

Once you have said no, never go back on it. Let your child know when you say no; you mean it. If you stand your ground with them, over time they will come to realise you mean "business."

Therefore, before you say no, be sure you are saying no to something you are 100% against your child doing.

All five steps will work but perseverance is needed.

Chapter Seven

Chapter Seven

The Power of Forgiveness (for parent and teen)

1. The Offence

2. The Hurt

3. I Forgive you

1 The Offence

Chapter seven addresses both parent and teen because both can cause offence to one another. From time to time, you will offend each other. Most day-to-day offences can blow over with not too much fuss and can be forgotten very quickly.

As you can see, this chapter is not as long as the others and that's because it doesn't need to be long. The sooner you can lay forgiveness on the table the better; it does not have to take years to forgive each other. Do it quickly and move on, it's better for everyone involved.

2 The Hurt

Some offences however may cause you or your teen deep hurt that can last for months, or worse, years. Hurt can come in all forms - harsh words, misunderstanding, a fight, loss of trust, and I'm sure you can add to this list. Hurt is real and can be deep rooted; it should never be swept under the carpet, or glossed over.

Discuss the hurt; let the person know what they did and how you feel about it. (Calmly)

3 I Forgive You

"I forgive you" can be the hardest words to say, but just like a seed in the ground it is better out than in. When you forgive, you are not saying you let the person off the hook, or what they did does not matter anymore, because a lot of the time; you have not let them off the hook and yes it does still matter.

However what forgiveness does is; it allows you to be free from the hold that the offence has had over you.

Sometimes you don't feel like forgiving the person who has hurt you. Forgiveness is not a feeling; it's a choice. And the sooner you choose to forgive, the sooner you start to heal.

Sometimes forgiveness needs to be two way; you forgiving them and them forgiving you,. But they don't want to forgive you. That's okay, as long as you have settled in your heart that you have forgiven them, that's the best you can do.

All three steps are a huge part of parenting. Master this and you can master anything.

In conclusion

Parenting goes hand in hand with life. Get your parenting right and your life has a better chance of going right.

I came across this poem and I thought it apt to conclude the ending of the book.

If a child lives with criticism, he learns to condemn.....

if a child lives with hostility, he learns to fight.....

If a child lives with fear, he learns to be apprehensive....

If a child lives with pity, he learns to feel sorry for himself......

If a child lives with ridicule, he learns to be shy.....

If a child lives with jealousy, he learns to feel guilt......

If a child lives with tolerance, he learns to be patient......

If a child lives with encouragement he learns to be confident....

If a child lives with praise, he learns to be appreciative......

If a child lives with acceptance, he learns to love......

If a child lives with honesty, he learns what truth is......

If a child lives with security, he learns to have faith.......

If a child lives with friendliness, he learns the world is a nice place in which to live.

Quotes for parents and by parents.

"The most important influence in my childhood was my father." DeForest Kelley

"My father was grounded a meat and potatoes man he was a baker". Anthony Hopkins

"I never had a speech from my father this is what you must do or shouldn't do, I just learned to led by example, my father wasn't perfect". Adam Sandler

"Being a mother is hard and it wasn't a subject I ever studied". Ruby Wax

"My father taught me the only way you can make good at anything is to practice and practice some more". Pete Rose

"Do you know that other than my father I've never had a man care for me" Dionne Warwick

"It was my father who taught me to value myself. He told me I was uncommonly beautiful and that I was the most precious thing in his life" Dawn French

"It is much easier to become a father than to be one". Kent Nerburn

"I hope I am remembered by my children as a good father". Orson Scott Card

"My father was a great teacher. But most of all he was a great dad". Reau Bridges

"It is easier for a father to have children than for children to have a real father". Pope XXIII

"Only God himself fully appreciates the influence of a Christian mother in the moulding of character in her children". Billy Graham

"When you are a mother you are really never alone in your thoughts. A mother always has to think twice, once for herself and once for her child" Sophie Loren

"The mother's heart is the child's classroom" Henry Ward Beecher

"The natural state of motherhood is unselfish. When you become a mother you are no longer the centre of your own universe. You relinquish that position to your children". Jessica Lange

"my mother was the most beautiful woman I ever saw. All I am, I owe to my mother. I attribute all my success in life to the moral intellectual and physical education I received from her". George Washington

"The human heart was not designed to beat outside the human body and yet your child represents just that, a parent's heart bared beating forever outside its chest" Debra Ginsberg

"Hugs can do great amounts of good especially for children" Diana, Princess of Wales.

"There can be no keener revelation of society's soul than the way in which it treats its children". Nelson Mandela

"While we try to teach our children all about life, our children teach us what life is all about". Angela Schwindt

"My heroes are and were my parents. I can't see having anyone else as my heroes". Michael Jordan

"Children are made readers on the laps of their parents". Emilie Buchwald

"A baby is God's opinion that the world should go on". Carl Sandburg

"To be in your children's memories tomorrow, you have to be in their lives today". Anonymous

"Everybody today seems to be in such a terrible rush, anxious for greater developments and greater riches and so on, so they have very little time for their parents. Parents have very little time for each other, and in the home begins the disruption of the peace of the world". Mother Theresa

"Parents need to fill a child's bucket with self-esteem so high that the world can't poke enough holes to drain it dry" Alvin Price

"Before I got married I had six theories about bringing up children; now I have six children and no theories".

John Wilmot

"Parenthood: It's about guiding the next generation, and forgiving the last". Peter Kruse

"We may not be able to prepare the future for our children, but we can at least prepare our children for the future". Franklin Roosevelt

"An alarming number of parents appear to have little confidence in the ability to teach their children. We should help parents understand the overriding importance of incidental teaching in the context of warm, consistent companionship. Such caring is usually the greatest teaching, especially if caring means sharing in the activities of the home". Raymond S Moore

"Our parents' prayers is the most beautiful poetry and expectations". Aditia Rinaldi

"Are parents always more ambitious for their children than they are for themselves". Jeffrey Archer

"Parents are not interested in JUSTICE; they are interested in PEACE and QUIET". Bill Cosby

"It's time for parents to teach young people early on that in diversity there is beauty and it is strength". Maya Angelou

"When I was a kid my parents moved a lot but I always found them". Rodney Dangerfield

"Parents have to instil the right principals in their children but it's up to the children to live up to those principals". Mary Lydon Simonsen

"Darkness cannot drive out darkness: only light can do that. Hate cannot drive out hate: only love can do that". Martin Luther King Jr.

www.amazingparenting.co.uk

More Books in the Amazing Parenting Collection

47455599R00068

Printed in Poland
by Amazon Fulfillment
Poland Sp. z o.o., Wrocław